CONTENTS

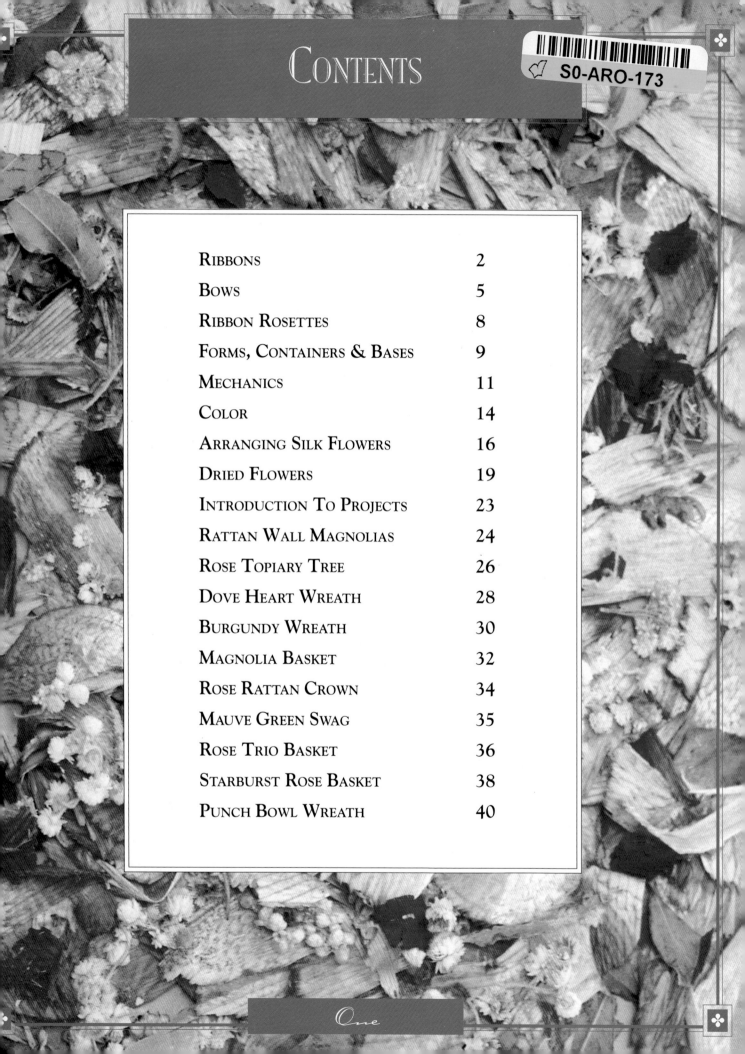

S0-ARO-173

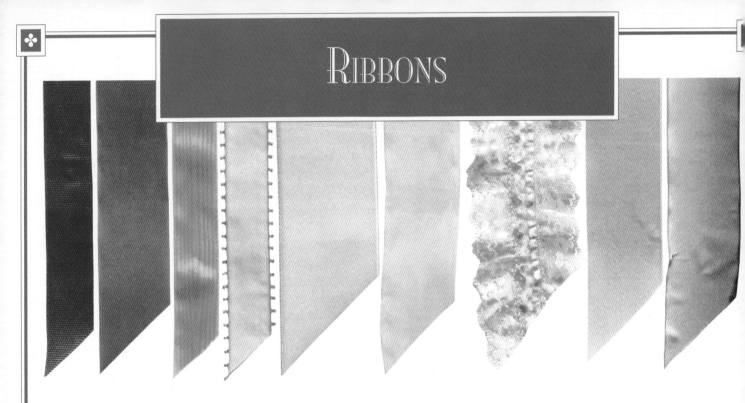

Ribbons

Ribbons create a feeling of elegant opulence and fanciful flights by softening angular shapes, gathering soft folds, nestling in small places and making sweeping gestures of texture and color. Some of the artful things to make with ribbons are very simple to create while others offer a little more challenge. With a little practice you can master them all.

Cotton– Casual, comfortable cotton is cut from bolt fabric and sized to maintain it's shape. Prints are usually one-sided; many stripes and plaids are considered two-sided, because they are woven. The ribbons found in craft stores are called cut-edge cotton. They can be cut lengthwise for narrower widths. Pleated cotton ribbons make interesting bows. Cottons are the most popular craft ribbons because they come in many beautiful patterns and colors.

Velvet–Elegant, rich velvet ribbons are made of a flock material. The colors and printed or embossed designs evoke images of celebrations and festivals. Velvet has a matte finish and is water resistant.

Satin–The most fluid of all ribbons, soft satins come in both cut-edge and woven-edge styles.

Cut-edge satin is less expensive, but it ravels along the lengthwise edges. Woven-edge satin ravels on the ends but not the sides. Woven-edge ribbons are usually washable but may shrink. They are water resistant.

Taffeta–Crisp, shiny, water-marked ribbons, very finely woven from silk or rayon have a cut edge. They make shapely, full-of-energy bows that hold their shape til you are ready for new ones.

Moire– Moire ribbon has a shimmering watermark finish. Stiff and substantial, it is well suited for making bows.

Burlap– Coarsely woven and heavily stiffened burlap can be made into bows that are subtle textured accents. Made of jute fibre, they lend a sturdy, comfortable, country feeling to a project.

Grosgrain and Faille–Richly-hued grosgrain and faille ribbons are made of woven blends and polyesters. Heavier than taffeta, they have delicate crosswise ribs-wider in grosgrain than in faille-creating a very subtle elasticity. Often used for trimming apparel, they both make shapely, lazy bows.

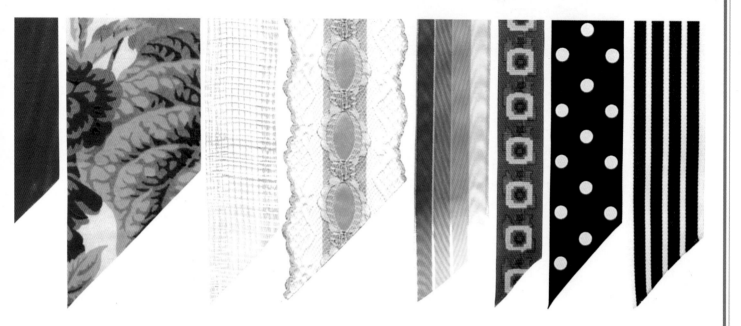

Lace–Floppy, lace bows have a mood of their own. They have finished edges and patterns that are often floral. Some ribbons have repeated perforations. Narrow ribbons can be threaded through to add extra sweetness or a color effect.

Piquot-edged–Piquot or feather edging is delicately looped threadwork. It appears on all types of ribbons and comes in prints or solid colors with lace edging or small trim on both sides.

French Wire Ribbon–Patterned and plain, opaque and silky sheer ribbons with tiny wire along the edges gives a new dimension to bows. Delicate bows hold their shape and heavier fabrics can be sculpted into dramatic designs.

Organdy– Gossamer, organdy ribbons can be either floppy or crisp. Some have beautiful silk-pattern trims.

Black and White– Ribbons take on graphic dimensions in black and white. They come in natural and polyester fabrics.

Outdoor Ribbon–Weatherproof ribbons are either plastic coated or made out of plastic material. They are perfect for porch centerpieces, hanging baskets, door decorations, and wreaths. Look for labels that recommend 'for outdoor use'.

Suggestions:

• Check manufacturer's directions before washing and allow for possible shrinkage.

• Use 24 gauge wire to secure center of bow. Twist as tightly as you can to make fluffy loops.

• Make larger loops and simpler bows when using coarse ribbons.

• Select fabrics and colors you are comfortable living with. When in doubt, choose natural.

• A glue gun can be very helpful when you don't seem to have enough fingers to hold ribbons and loops in place when making bows.

Streamers

They can link bows, plates, pictures etc. together or enhance and balance a bow; they can be draped in a pattern, looped or decorated and hung down a narrow wall. Streamers are the symbol of celebrations.

To attach streamers to a bow, cut a length of ribbon proportioned to fit bow and long enough for both streamers. Hold the two cut ends together and angle cut as desired. Attach center of streamers to center of bow with floral wire on the back.

Twisters

Twisters are a way to add a bouncy, splash of color to a plant or a present. Acetate or taffeta ribbons make the best twisters.

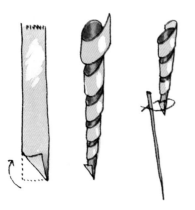

1. Cut a 10" piece of #9 ribbon. Fold one end up as shown in the illustration. Hold one end in your left hand while twisting the other end tightly with your right hand. The ribbon will form a spiral shape.

2. Wrap the ribbon ends with wire or floral tape and attach to wooden floral picks.

3. Cover the wooden picks with floral tape.

Loops

The symmetry and precision of bows are impressive, but loops combined with streamers provide a decorative style of their own. They can be made out of anything from silk to raffia, and once you know the basics you can embellish to suit the project or occasion.

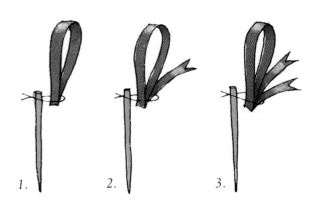

1.   2.   3.

1. To form a plain loop, use size #5 or #9 ribbon. Cut ribbon piece about 5" long. Bringing cut ends together, fold with right side of ribbon out. Gather ends around wooden floral pick and secure with wire.

2. To form a loop with a tail use extra ribbon. Cut end of streamer with one of the cut options.

3. To make a loop with two tails, cut a length of ribbon 10" long. Starting at the middle of the ribbon, fold in half with wrong sides together. Fold each side of doubled ribbons over again forming two tails. Pinch ribbon together at these last folds and secure with wire to wooden floral pick. Trim ends as desired.

Single Loop Bow

The single loop bow can be used for centerpieces, wreaths, tree boughs, dress collars, hats, sashes, live plants, napkin rings etc. It is the easiest bow to make if many are needed.

You can vary the basic single loop bow by adding extra tails, staggering the length of the tails, or exaggerating the diameter.

1. Cross ribbon ends making 4" tails. Where the ribbons cross is the center of the bow.

2. Bring the center together with the crossed ribbons. Pinch ribbons together and secure with a small piece of florist wire.

3. Cut tails at an angle or in points to finish.

4. Add decorative detail to center with glue gun or wire.

Florist Bow

1. Hold the ribbon right side up between thumb and index finger. Pinch the ribbon 4" from end and form a loop as large as you need, rolling the ribbon up and away from you. Place the long end of the ribbon between thumb and index finger to create the bow's center.

2. Make a half twist to the left so ribbon will be right side out and make bottom loop by rolling the ribbon down and away from you. Pinch the ribbon together at the bow center.

3. Continue making loops keeping loop sizes the same.

4. Before securing bow with wire, add button loop to top by twisting the end of the tail on top of the bow, (making sure the right side is out) over and under your thumb. Place wire through the small center loop, taking care to secure the end, and twist.

5. Arrange loops to form bow.

6. Cut desired length of ribbon to create a tie for the bow and place tie through the small center loop and knot in back.

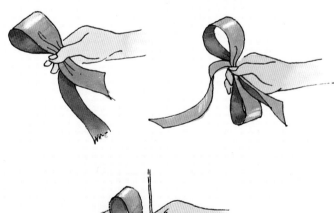

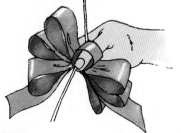

Size Guide for Single Loop Bow

Ribbon Size	Diameter of Bow with 4" tails	Yardage required
5	6"	5/8 yd.
9	7"	3/4 yd.
40	9"	1 yd.

BOWS

All-purpose Bow

Shoelaces were probably the first bow you ever learned to make. Once that was mastered all kinds of opportunities opened up for you to try out your new skill: packages, dresses, ponytails...the list goes on. Here is how to make the perfect, all-purpose bow.

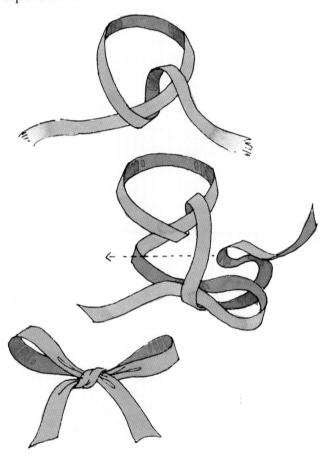

Fluffy Bow

An average size fluffy bow can be made with about 3 1/2 yds. of ribbon. The fluffy bow is a traditional gift wrap bow.

1. Wrap all the ribbon around fingers of right hand.

2. Hold the wrapped ribbon together at the center with one hand and cut two notches as shown.

3. Tie the center tightly with a short piece of ribbon or a twist of wire.

4. Spread the loops into a fluffy round bow.

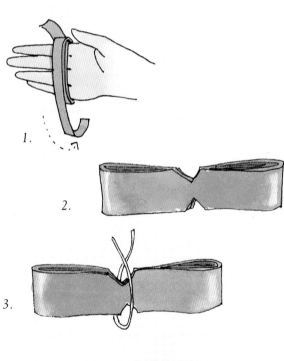

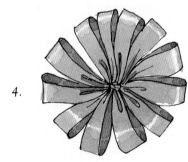

1. Starting with both ends even, cross the right ribbon underneath the left and make a half knot.

2. Keeping wrong sides of the ribbon together, make a loop between the thumb and index finger of the left hand.

3. Cross over the top of the loop with the ribbon right side up.

4. Finish second loop by pulling it up through the center space you've just created and pull tightly.

Three-loop Crisscross Bow

A regal looking bow that makes up nicely in double-faced satin looks great mounted on a wall over a picture (as shown) or any 'important look-ing' place. You will need three lengths of ribbon: one twenty-five inch and one fifty-inch length of 4 5/8" wide ribbon and a ten inch length of 1 1/2" wide ribbon. Note: For a contrasting edge, bind wider ribbon with different color, narrow ribbon after measuring.

1. Lay shorter piece of wide ribbon flat. Bring ends into center overlapping slightly.

2. Pleat at center and bind with florist's wire. Find center of longer piece, form a loop and bind with wire.

3. Iron a narrow ribbon in half lengthwise and place a short bow across the top of the long one below the loop.

4. Crisscross a narrow ribbon around the bow center.

5. Pull tightly to bind and stitch at back. Trim the ends evenly.

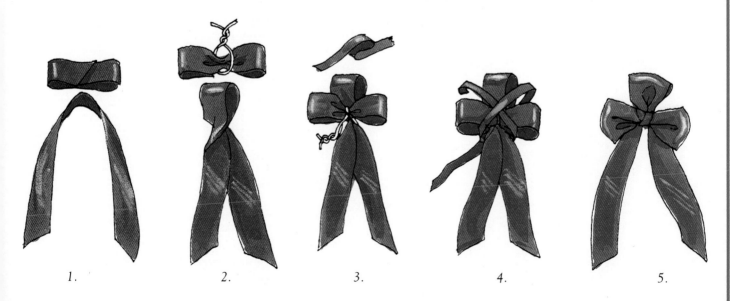

1.   2.   3.   4.   5.

Ribbon Rosettes

A bouquet of satin rosettes wired together and stitched to a wide ribbon gently gathers a gossamer curtain or the corners of a flower-filled canopy adding a feeling of gentleness and caring to special places in your home. Supple, satin ribbon works best for making rosettes which can also be sewn onto hats and dresses or hot glued on top of packages. When making a mature blossom, start with seven feet of 2 1/2" wide ribbon. (A bud requires four feet of 1" wide ribbon.)

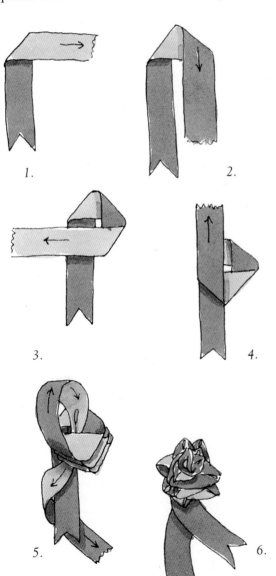

1. Lay ribbon on a flat surface and fold over at a ninety degree angle leaving five inches free at end.

2. Make another ninety degree fold working in a clockwise direction.

3. Repeat. Ribbon will form a square.

4. Continue folding ribbon clockwise on itself in a square pattern until you have built up four complete layers.

5. Slide pile onto one hand and push loose ribbon end down through center hole with other hand.

6. With free hand, twist the loose ribbon clockwise from below to make the folded ribbon squares start forming petals.

7. Bind tightly below petals with florist wire. Trim loose ends.

Storing Your Ribbons

The accomplished bow maker, like any artist, will find many opportunities to practice her or his skill. Eventually the question of where and how to keep the growing number of beautiful ribbons organized is bound to come up. A good way to keep them safe, orderly, and readily available is to hang them on a wall in a dry place away from sunlight. They tend to fade. Their decorative appearance will be both pleasing and inspiring.

- Expandable hat racks (verticle or horizontal)
- Coat racks (verticle or horizontal)
- Paper towel holders
- Towel holders
- Wooden drapery rods
- Rain gutters (Have a lumberyard cut a half-round gutter and cap the ends. Punch holes along the top edge and mount.)

Forms, Containers and Bases

They transcend their useful purpose and become an artistic component of design, an integral part of it. The only practical requirement for containers, forms and bases is that they be sturdy enough to balance the weight and breadth of the selected, arrangement material.

Abstract forms, like interesting driftwood or graceful branches, are distinguished by size, color and texture; the whole makes a pattern in space. Forms can be used with or without containers.

Driftwood form

Flowering trees and shrubs such as: dogwood, tree lilac, star magnolia, pear and quince have well-shaped, bare branches for arrangements. Many can be found along the road after a storm or during tree removals.

Wood forms found inland usually need considerable grooming. Partially decayed and covered with dirt, they require strong hosing, scraping with a stiff wire brush and chisel, or soaking and scrubbing with soap and water. Sanding the surface improves the texture; varnish, stain or wax enhances grain and color.

Carved by wind, water and rock driftwood may emerge as a completed work of art; clean and shining, it needs no refinement. Or, a shape may be altered by removing some of the portions and relocating them to improve the height or balance. Segments may be added to increase size, or when combining two or more pieces, to produce a more complex form.

Although the finish seldom needs retouching, the surface highlights may be enhanced by shading with pastel chalk, which can be washed off if you don't like the effect. A light application of clear plastic spray will protect the wood and make it easier to clean.

As sculptural characteristics become visible, the form can be studied from all sides to determine possible reshaping and mounting. If sections need to be removed and relocated, epoxy glue is a good bonding agent. Metal rods or sections of wire coat hangers can also join segments. Inserted into holes drilled into the wood and properly fitted, segments can be joined without gluing.

Collect a few standard containers; a shallow bowl, cylinder, compote, goblet, trough shape, oval, basket, urn...look for the unusual. Since it doesn't have to be watertight, the choices can range from a tiny shell for a miniature arrangement to a large stone urn for a large room or impressive building.

Containers should be suitable for the setting and complement the atmosphere of the room. Baskets blend especially well with either vibrant or muted shades of flowers and are well suited to informal settings and country-style furnishings.

Containers

Forms, Containers, & Bases

A base of slate or a cross-cut of wood can be used as a platform to work from and can also contribute to the shape and mood of the design. For a more formal arrangement the wood can be covered with velvet, and for a less formal style with a sturdy fabric such as burlap. Polished or unpolished wood, cork, bamboo, clear plastic sheets, blocks of plexiglass and polished marble are all excellent and versatile materials for bases.

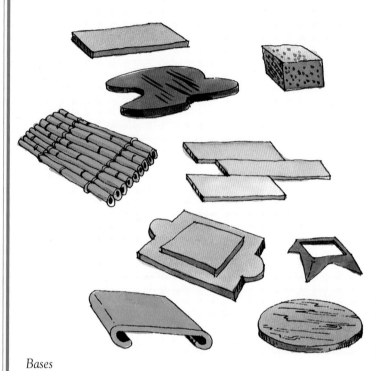

Bases

Crescent shape design in a candle cup

Brass, copper silver and pewter can be beautiful complements to arrangements and come in a variety of sizes, shapes and functions. Wrought ironwork can also add a distinctive look to flowers and foliage.

Goblets, wine glasses, builders glass bricks, modern glass sculptures and a variety of glass vases are all attractive material for silk flower arrangements.

The plumbing department of your local hardware store is a goldmine for interesting shapes and sizes. PVC pipe can be hot glued onto a wooden base and fashioned into unusual containers.

Old earthenware jars, ovenware, hand-thrown pottery, clay drainage pipes and ornate china also make interesting containers for flower arrangements.

Just as there is no end to pretty things, there is no end to pretty things to put them in.

The mainstay of any floral design is the device that holds it together. Anchors to support an arrangement of silk flowers must be firmly secured and inconspicuous.

Florist Foam

Absorbent foam is stuffed inside, or plastic foam is adhered to the bottom of your container, and the flowers and dried materials are inserted into it. Floral foam comes in rounds, sticks or blocks of various styles and sizes. It can easily be cut to the appropriate size with a knife or small saw.

Light stems will stay where they are placed in the foam, but the long or heavy stems may tend to swivel. This can be avoided by slitting the tape which binds a multi-wired stem and separating the wires into a fork, which is pushed into the foam.

For a single-wire stem, another wire is twisted around the base of the stem to form an extra 'leg' or, if the stem is relatively short, you can add a dollop of tacky glue in the hole where the stem pokes into the foam.

Extra leg

Plastic foam is a coarse, non-porous foam. It's a good choice for working with large silk flowers. It can be cut to shape and wedged into a container or anchored to the bottom with clay or hot glue.

Desert foam is also coarse and non-porous and is easier to penetrate than plastic foam.

Sahara foam is a finer, non-porous foam which is generally used with fresh and dry materials, because it is easy to penetrate and will not break fragile stems.

Oasis foam is highly absorbent and used to maintain fresh plants. It can also be used as a filler for tall vases and when combining fresh and silk flowers.

Terms and tools

A plastic frog is a circle of plastic (which is glued to the bottom of the container or base) with several upright prongs on which foam is impaled.

A foam anchor has a heavy metal base with long, widely-spaced pins similar in function to a plastic frog.

A well pinholder is a small container with vertical pins inside. Pinholders are helpful when combining fresh and fabric flowers, including natural and dried foliage with heavy stems. To support the wire stems of the silk flowers, attach a small piece of sahara foam over the pins on part of the pinholder.

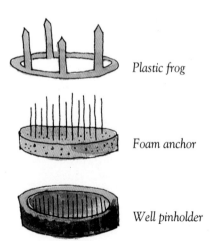

Plastic frog

Foam anchor

Well pinholder

Floral tape is available in a variety of colors, floral tape sticks to itself and is used to wrap around wire flower stems.

Floral wire, a green enameled wire, 18,20 or 22 gauge is used to extend stems or support flowers cut from original stems. The higher the gauge number, the thinner the wire. *See pg. 13.*

Floral adhesive tape is a special tape available for securing foam. The double-sided tape used for covering wire stems can also be used for securing foam.

Waterproof clay that is non-drying and reusable is also used to anchor plastic frogs, well pinholders and foam anchors. Make sure the surface is absolutely dry and free of dust or the clay won't stick.

Candlecup

Small, inexpensive containers known as 'candlecups' are designed to fit on candlesticks and can also be fitted into the necks of bottles. Comparable to a needle-holder, a cupholder is a small receptacle and needle-holder welded together. Though shallow, a cupholder can accommodate a sizable arrangement. A cupholder centered on a candlestick converts it to a container when the two are attached with floral clay or tied with florist wire (22 gauge). They are available in various sizes and are made in chrome, brass, copper and white or colored plastic. *See pg. 10.*

Hiding the Anchors

Reindeer moss soaked until it is soft and pliable can be placed over the foam before the flowers are inserted. *Flora and fauna* can be arranged near the rim of the container to conceal the supports. *Spaghnum moss*, the kind you find growing on the ground, rocks or at the base of trees, *Spanish moss*, a string-like moss that grows on trees in the South, or *bulb fibre* can also be used to disguise the mechanics. Greening pins, 'u' shaped or hairpin-like, wire pins can be inserted through moss and dried material and into the floral foam to hold it in place.

Stones, driftwood or pebbles also make good camoflage. In modern, free-form arrangements the foam can be coloured to match the container or base with paint from an aerosol spray can.

Mechanics For Tall Containers

Oasis foam and scraps of plastic foam can be salvaged, cut into small pieces and stuffed inside a container to hold flowers in place. Foam need not be moistened when used to hold silk and dried flowers.

Fillers such as sand, Kitty Litter or even bird gravel can be used to raise the floor of the container closer to the top. If the container tends to topple over you can add marbles or sand to the bottom for ballast.

Other Mechanics for Holding Flowers in Place

1. Crumpled turkey wire

2. Lead cross-bar sling

3. Scotch tape (for delicate flowers)

4. One-inch chicken wire basket

Crumpled turkey wire

Oasis sticks

Lead crossbar sling

1" chicken wire basket

Scotch tape

Rewiring Silk Flowers and Adding Wire Stems To Dried Flowers

Having control over the length of the stem is a great advantage in flower arranging. We can always shorten a stem, but with silk and dried materials we can also lengthen and strengthen them. Leaves and longer stems can be added to the inexpensive silk flowers, called picks, which are available on short wire stems.

When a flower stem has two or more blossoms, to have more control over your design, cut off the blossoms and give each flower head a new stem.

Here is how to do it.

Basic Tools
• 20 gauge wire
• Needle-nose pliers
• Small wire cutter
• Green floral tape

1. Cut each flower head from the spray so that the stem is approximately 1 1/2" long.

2. Using 20 gauge wire, cut wire to the desired length, allowing extra for bending and for the part of the stem to be inserted into the floral foam. Bend tip of wire with pliers to form a 'shepherd's hook'.

1 1/2"

3. Hook wire around the calyx, where the flower head joins the stem, and squeeze tightly with needle-nose pliers.

4. Wrap green floral tape over wire from top to bottom.

Imagine a world without color; a white sun and moon distinguishable by brightness; objects, people and places defined in black, white and grey.

Would life be simpler or more dramatic; would words like 'luscious','sensuous', 'delicious', 'vibrant', 'brilliant' and 'warm' have meaning to us? There is more to color than meets the eye.

When light hits a red apple on the table, only the red rays are reflected into our eyes, and we say 'red'. The color we see is always the one being reflected, the one that doesn't stay put and get absorbed. We see the reflected color and say 'an apple is red'. But in truth an apple is everything but red.

When the light is diminished we still perceive the red apple as red. We are not cameras; our eyes do not just measure wavelengths of light. We remember color; we store memories of color and tend to see the same ones the same way. We also judge colors by the company they keep. We compare them to one another and revise according to the time of day, light source and memory. The eye works with ratios of color, not with absolutes.

Do we all see colors the same way?

Are there simple, perceptual color truths that people share? Most people can identify between 150 and 200 colors. But we do not all see exactly the same colors, especially if we're color-blind. Animals perceive colors differently fromthe way we do, depending on their chemistry, and many see only in black and white. Some respond to colors invisible to us, but to use color to make life more meaningful is unique to humans.

Color is in the eyes of the beholder

Color doesn't occur in the world, but in the mind. Scientists have known for years that certain colors trigger an emotional response in people. Children will use dark colors to express their sadness when painting and bright colors to express happiness. During the 60's the vibrational aspect of colors was tested in various countries. People with blindfolds identified colors by touch, some were warmer or cooler than others. Some colors felt more 'lively' or more 'calm'.

In recent years there have been books written about color therapy, and color consultants tell us which colors the body needs to feel more balanced, harmonious and 'normal'.

Within each of us is a natural desire for color. We crave it like we long for the sun in the middle of winter. It comforts us on many levels.

The choice is yours.

Our color choices come from a personal point of view; we have emphatic preferences and prejudices. There are no wrong colors or reasons for choosing some over others; colors offer complete freedom of choice. Whatever is pleasing to us is right for us. If our choice is different from someone elses we are reminded to appreciate the differences.

Colors can be warm or cold; oranges, yellows and reds are warm and welcoming. They are a lift to the spirit when placed in dark corners and hallways. Cool colors like blue, white, grey and some greens, the colors of ice and sea, have a calming effect. When cool colors are placed where they will be seen from a distance they tend to recede. Warm colors reach out to greet us; cool colors shy away.

The placement of colors in an arrangement produces a specific effect in a majority of people. For instance: dark shades in the lower areas provide a weighted feeling at the bottom; and bright colors that attract more attention, if featured in the center, will create a focus. Light, airy hues give a lift to a design if placed at the top and edges. This is a traditional color composition although modern design often breaks conventional practices.

Analogous or neutralized colors that are muted in

hue are probably the most popular when creating combinations because they are more reconciled by the eye than complementary ones with their sharp differences. Containers in bright colors can be very dramatic but are often too eye-catching and detract from the arrangement. This can be avoided by repeating the container color in the choice of flowers. A pure white container is a dominant element, but the addition of some white flowers to the arrangement provides a balancing link.

Monochromatic themes can be interesting because they encompass the full range of only one color. Repetition of shades of color create a fluid, rhythmical effect and can be restful and contemplative.

Some flower arrangers prefer the sharp contrasts of opposite colors; others prefer muted tints, tones and shade. Either way a color sense is developed through an awareness of the colors around us, and our choices expand as we gain familiarity with different combinations.

Less can be more.

Picasso was quoted as saying that if he felt comfortable painting with three colors, he would use two; and if he felt at ease with two he would use one.

A riot of color may be exhilarating to play with for awhile but not easy to live with over a period of time. When a project is made for the home, the color of the walls influences the colors and elements in the project. Decide where your project is going to hang or sit; be aware of the colors in the rest of the room and the light source before selecting the materials. Color and texture should be considered when you are creating and positioning an arrangement because they tend to influence an atmosphere or mood.

Creative impulse can find a direction in the use of color to express moods, occasions, characteristics such as: joy, celebration, rustic or delicate, and sometimes projects can also find a theme in 'purely decorative'.

ARRANGING SILK FLOWERS

*S*ilk flowers is the generic name for several styles of silk, polyester and paper flowers. There are freeze-dried silk flowers that look like dried flowers yet have the durability of fabric; there are beautiful, subtle shades of paper flowers and flowers made of vinyl that have a sturdy appearance and velvety soft petals that look and feel similar to fresh blooms. Prices vary from 49 cents to 5o dollars for a single rose...something for everyone. Many brands of 'ozone friendly' sprays to clean silk and dried flowers have made it possible to recycle arrangements for years.

Horizontal Design

Although fresh flowers inspire us to touch their soft petals, smell their unique perfumes and make them our own, they do not compare to silk ones because silk flowers offer a different range of possibilities. They can be shaped, lengthened, combined with natural and unusual objects and placed or hung in places not favorable for cut or growing flowers and foliage. Just as fresh flowers will always charm and delight us, silk flowers have come into their own as a pleasing art form to decorate the home or office.

Helpful Hints for Standard Designs

1. Cut oasis or plastic foam to fit inside of container snugly, but let it reach 1 to 2 inches above the rim so you can insert flowers to glide sideways or gracefully around the top. Use filler material to hide stems and mechanics. *See pg. 12.*

2. Position a container with three legs to show one leg directly in front.

3. Set straight stalks at different angles to vary directions.

4. Insert flowers of the same length at different angles to avoid placements at the same height.

5. To create depth, place some flowers behind others.

6. Allow breathing space between flowers to prevent a crowded look.

7. Place lacy flowers, small sizes and pale shades at top and outer areas.

8. Group flowers of the same type to avoid a scattered, spotty effect.

9. Dark colors and heavy flowers will give a sense of stability if placed in lower central area.

10. Use flowers in different stages of development from bud to full bloom.

Centerpieces

Select a container that is suitable in size, shape and character; formal or informal according to the setting. Wicker looks better with pottery and plastic; and silver and crystal look better with china. The container should suit the design and color of the place settings. If the dishes are colorful, select most of the arranging material in the hue that appears in the smallest quantity in the china.

Flowers can be a way of unifying a table by bringing the color together and creating a special feeling. Arrangements shouldn't be so high that they interfere with eating or conversation; and they shouldn't spread out among the dishes and utensils. Because the arrangement will be viewed from all sides, be aware of designing from a pivotal point, sometimes called a 'central axis'. It is the point from which all stems, branches and filler material are angled.

Seventeen

Styles and designs

There are eight different ways to structure a flower arrangement; but in each of these, the use of scale and choice of colors, containers and textures provides many variations.

1. *Horizontal* arrangements are often used for table or windowsill decorations. The focal point is the center. Stems radiate in all directions. *See pg. 16*

2. *Vertical* arrangements have a strong, upward movement and may be a tall, narrow triangle or a simple line of flowers about twice the height of the container. Iris, arum lily or bird of paradise flowers are often used. The stems of a vertical arrangement originate from many points. *See pg. 15.*

3. *Triangular* arrangements create the basic form of the triangle and gradually fill in with materials of varying lengths and sizes. The shape may be equally balanced on each or asymmetrical with one point of the triangle extending further than the other. A variety of size, shape and texture in the flowers is used. Stems radiate from a central point, usually wth paler and smaller flowers and leaves at the outer edges graduating to larger, deep-colored or brighter blooms at the center. *See right.*

4. The *crescent* arrangement may be symmetrical or asymmetrical, the focal point being created at the base of the main stems. Candlesticks provide an elegant base for an inverted crescent or a double curve in the form of an 's' shape. The flexible, wiry stems of silk flowers can be smoothed into curves with a gentle pressure of thumbs and forefingers. *See pg. 10.*

5. The *circular or oval* arrangement has a similar appearance from all sides. It can be constructed in a formal way with larger blooms centrally placed and smaller ones echoing around the edges, or one of my favorites is something that looks like a large handful of blooms, grasped from a flower-covered field, that settle into a generous container and spread out like a giant oak tree. Casual look-ing bouquets look easy to do but require patiently placing many many small flowers allowing for spaces in-between. *See pg. 17.*

6. *Minimal* arrangements make use of space as an element, and styling is done with an economy of materials. The effectiveness of the arrangement often relies on contrasts of texture, form and color.

7. *Still life* designs incorporate a variety of objects. Some arrangements represent a natural setting such as the countryside, seashore, a garden, or in more modern arrangements, sculpture, or high-tech items. A base of slate or unpolished wood is often used with the container hidden from view.

8. *Wall-hanging* arrangements designed in baskets that are made like sconces are seen from the front and either side. With stems radiating from a central point, a variety of sizes, shapes and textures can fill the basket and flow over the sides. The basket can be a contrast against the wall or can be spray painted to blend in.

Triangular arrangement.

DRIED FLOWERS

Like silk flowers, dried flowers have a charm of their own. Combining flowers from different seasons, they make lovely bouquets; and when designed and framed; glued or pinned to ribbons and added to hats, and preserved as bridal bouquets, they remind us of fragrant, warm, sunny days and special times in our life. There are many time-honored ways to preserve flowers and plants.

1. They can be dried between sheets of absorbent paper that is inserted between the pages of a thick book. In two to three weeks, the weight of the book will press out the plant moisture which is absorbed by the paper.

2. Flowers can be tied together in small bunches and hung upside down in a cool, dark place until dry.

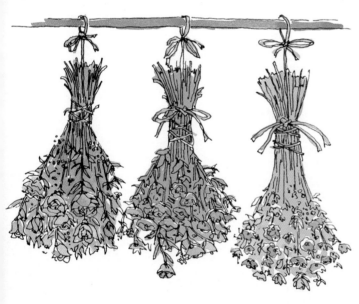

3. Desiccants such as silica gel, borax and yellow cornmeal can be used to dry flowers by cutting off the heads (wire stems are added) and covering them with a blanket of silica gel or an equal mixture of borax and cornmeal for a week. Desiccants often work better for delicate flowers because the flowers can be wired before drying. *See pg. 13.*

But the newest and fastest way to dry flowers is the microwave method. The heat of the microwave evaporates the moisture in a flower or leaf, and this moisture is then absorbed by the silica gel.

Silica Gel

Silica gel has a strong absorbing property. It is ideal for drying flowers because the small granules easily penetrate even the most delicate flower heads. It's sold in garden shops, drugstores, craft shops and floral shops.

Silica gel can spread a fine dust particle that can be irritating to the mucus membranes. Work in well ventilated areas.

When dry, silica gel is blue, but the granules become a whitish-pink color as they absorb moisture. You can tell when the silica granules have reached their saturation point by checking the color. Silica gel can be re-used for years by removing the moisture from the granules each time they become saturated.

Restoring Silica Gel for Re-use

OVEN METHOD

1. Pre-heat oven to 300 degrees. Sift through the silica gel to remove as much leftover plant material as possible. Spread a single layer of silica gel evenly on the bottom of a shallow pan, and place it uncovered in the oven.

2. Stir every so often and watch for the return of the original blue color.

3. Cool completely and store in a tight-fitting, covered container.

ON THE STOVE

1. Place uncovered in a low, wide frying pan (non-teflon).

2. Heat on medium heat, while stirring granules from time to time until they become blue again.

3. When blue and cool, store as described above.

DRIED FLOWERS

IN THE MICROWAVE

1. Spread in an open cardboard box or microwavable dish and place on a rack in the microwave.

2. Set microwave at medium high or high for about ten minutes. Interrupt to stir every few minutes.

3. When blue and cool, store as described above.

How to Dry Flowers in Your Microwave

Choose flowers that are partially opened. Petals fall off if the flower is in full bloom. Buds will not dry well because the silica gel cannot find its way to the tighly closed petals in the center. Some small buds can be dried however; experiment. Leaves are dried separately because they dry faster. Select simple-structured flowers like marigolds for your first flower. Let the dew dry on the petals and leaves before microwaving.

In principle all flowers can be dried, but flowers with thick petals such as: clematis vitelba, hyacinth, iris and magnolia do not dry well even in the micro-wave. Each flower and leaf has its own unique drying time, so avoid placing different varieties in the microwave at the same time.

Most flowers hold their shape better if dried face-up. Branches with multiple blossoms, however, should be dried lying flat.

When drying face-up, cut stem leaving a generous inch from head. A floral wire stem can be added after drying by attaching it to the stem and covering it with floral tape. *See pg. 13.*

Toothpicks can be inserted next to or through the stem of delicate flowers. The wire can be wrapped around the toothpick or poked through the flower head, hooked over a portion of the head, pulled back through and tightened after it's dried.

If petals are folded over one another, like petals on some roses, remove them before drying so the silica gel can reach the inner petals. (Use tweezers.)

1. Layer 1 1/4" of silica gel on the bottom of your container with a spoon.

2. Place flowers or leaves on top leaving 1 1/4" between the sides of the container and individual flowers.

3. Sprinkle silica gel around the plant edges and add another 1 1/4" layer of silica gel on top.

4. Place uncovered container on rack or elevated in the microwave.

Drying Time and Temperature

Because of the variation in microwaves and the amount of moisture in plants its impossible to give exact guidelines. Generally speaking, drying time for one or more flowers and leaves in about 1/2 pound of silica gel is 2 to 2 1/2 minutes; 2 1/4 pounds of silica gel, 5 to 6 minutes; and 3 1/2 pounds of silica gel, 6 to 7 minutes at a 300 watts setting.

If you are not sure of the temperature setting on your microwave, insert a non-metal thermometer between the flowers in the silica gel positioned so you can read it through the door. Stop 'cooking' when the silica gel reaches 300 degrees.

To prevent moisture forming and being re-absorbed by the flowers after they have been dried, put a lid over flowers and allow them to remain standing in the microwave for 10 to 15 minutes with the door open. They will continue drying even after the oven is turned off.

Gently remove the flowers. Using a small paint-brush, lightly remove remaining silica gel. If some continues to cling to the petals, store flowers in a tightly-closed box, and the silica gel will eventually fall off.

If some parts of the stem or flower are still damp, cover those parts with silica gel and return flowers to microwave for a minute, repeating the covered standing time. Allow the silica gel to cool in-between drying batches of flowers.

GENERAL GUIDELINES

Sellecting Your Materials

This is the most important part of a floral design. If you want to match another item, be sure to take samples with you when you select your materials. Choose things you can live with. When in doubt about which colors to use, it's better to go natural.

Filler Flowers

Babies' breath, tweedia, alstromeria, daisies, bell flowers and wild flowers all have a pleasing effect in a floral. Let some of your materials spill out of the arrangement and onto the table around your design.

Make Your Own Bird Nest

Hold a small amount of Spanish moss in one hand. Twist the other hand in the center of the moss to hollow out slightly. Don't make it too neat.

Raffia Loops

Start with one end of the raffia strip and make loops the size you need for where you want to put it. Use all of strip ending with a piece about 2 to 4" long. Hold together with wire as shown.

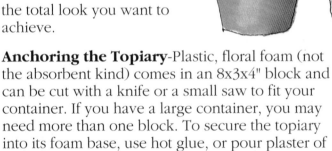

Topiary Trees

Selecting Topiaries-Consider the height of the tree when making your selection. Taller topiaries (30" and higher) make elegant decorations for mantels and doorways. Smaller topiaries (18-20") are more suitable for tables.

Containers-Terra cotta, brass, ceramic, wood, lattice and wicker all make beautiful containers for topiaries. Coordinate your choice of container with the total look you want to achieve.

Anchoring the Topiary-Plastic, floral foam (not the absorbent kind) comes in an 8x3x4" block and can be cut with a knife or a small saw to fit your container. If you have a large container, you may need more than one block. To secure the topiary into its foam base, use hot glue, or pour plaster of paris around the foam base.

Decorating topiaries-Both silk and dried flowers make beautiful topiary trees. Some of the most popular decorating choices are roses and small wild flowers. Dried material, birds and berries are excellent accent items and coordinate with most other materials. Select the appropriate type of ribbon to achieve the finished look: satin ribbon gives a Victorian and English garden look while sinamay ribbon, burlap, raffia and paper ribbon create a natural, country effect.

Finishing Touches-To cover the foam base use Spanish moss, sheet moss, excelsior or greenery such as: boxwood ivy, or choose from a variety of short greenery picks. Consider the overall look of the design when you cover the foam base.

Rattan Wall Magnolias

Materials

- ❖ 1 – 22" Natural Round Rattan Wall Piece
- ❖ 2 – Ivory Grand Magnolias w/ Leaves
- ❖ 11 – 18" Natural Pheasant Tail Feathers
- ❖ 3 yds.– Natural Paper Ribbon
- ❖ Small Amount – Natural Statice
- ❖ 1 oz.– Natural Raffia
- ❖ 1 oz. – Spanish Moss
- ❖ 1 Pkg. – Green Eucalyptus
- ❖ 2 – Lotus Pods
- ❖ Glue (hot glue recommended)

Instructions

1 Untwist paper ribbon. Make a 12" florist bow (*see page 5*). Glue at bottom of wreath .

2 Cut large outer petals from one magnolia and keep closed for bud.

3 Arrange magnolias, magnolia leaves, lotus pods and feathers as shown.

4 Fill in with eucalyptus, statice and raffia loops. *See page 23.*

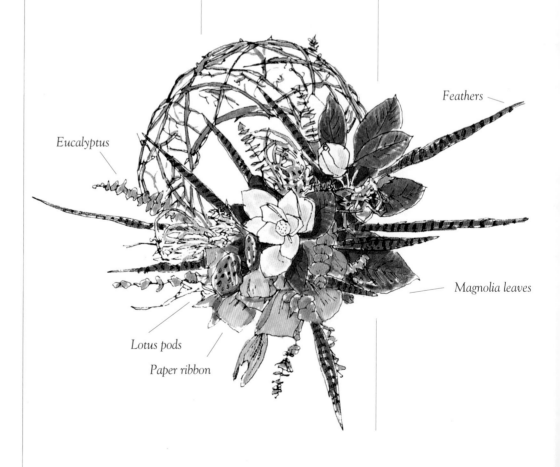

Feathers

Eucalyptus

Magnolia leaves

Lotus pods

Paper ribbon

Rose Topiary Tree

Materials

- *1 – 18" Natural Rattan Topiary Tree*
- *1 – 5 1/2" White Lattice Wood Planter*
- *2 yards – 1 3/8" Pink/ White, Wired Ribbon*
- *8 – 1" Pink Dried Open Roses*
- *20 – 1" Pink Dried Rosebuds*
- *1 Stem Mini Ivy Vine*
- *1/2 oz. – Spanish Moss*
- *1 – Floral Foam Block*
- *Glue (hot glue recommended)*

Instructions

1 Cut foam block to fit in bottom of lattice planter. Glue to secure

2 Glue topiary tree trunk into center of foam. Fill around base with Spanish moss as shown. Glue as needed.

3 Glue one end of a 27" length of ribbon to top of tree, loop and curl ribbon down and around trunk. Glue other end to corner of planter, as shown.

4 Make two 4" fluffy bows from pink ribbon (*see page 6*). Glue one to top of tree and the other to corner of planter over ends of ribbon length.

5 Cut ivy vine into small sections. Glue ivy leaves, roses and rosebuds to tree around bows.

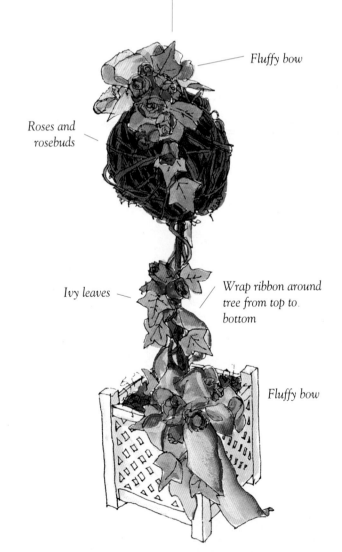

Fluffy bow

Roses and rosebuds

Ivy leaves

Wrap ribbon around tree from top to bottom

Fluffy bow

Suggested uses: As a center table piece, in an entry hall on a dressing table or on a sofa table.

Dove Heart Wreath

Materials

- ❖ 1– 30" Wild Birch Trailing Heart
- ❖ 2 – 2 1/4" Lavender Sitting Doves
- ❖ 3 – 3" Plumb/Green Raspberry Picks
- ❖ 1/2 Yd. – 1 3/8" Cranberry Wired Ribbon
- ❖ 1/4 Yd. 6" White Tulle Net
- ❖ Small Amount – Spanish Moss
- ❖ Glue (hot glue recommended)

Instructions

1 Glue a "nest" of Spanish moss at base of heart. Glue additional amounts of moss randomly around heart and trailing portion of wreath, as shown.

2 Using wired ribbon, make a 4 1/2" florist bow (*see page 5*). Glue bow beneath "nest". Add a small amount of moss to center of bow, gluing to secure.

3 Arrange and glue doves into moss "nest" as shown.

4 Cut berry pick into eight smaller sections. Glue one section at center of bow and remaining sections into moss around wreath. Refer to drawing.

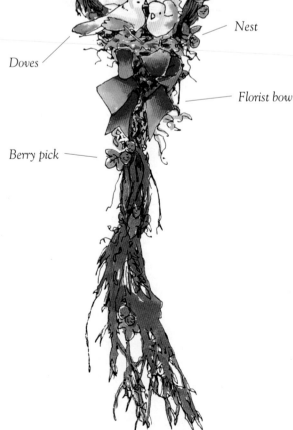

Wild birch trailing heart

Nest

Doves

Florist bow

Berry pick

Twenty nine

BURGUNDY WREATH

Materials

- 1 – 24" *Natural Grapevine Wreath*
- 3 *Stems – Burgundy Open Roses*
- 2 *Stems – Burgundy Rosebuds*
- 3 *Stems – 22" Minuet Rambling Rose*
- 3 *Stems – 17" Plumb/ Green, Berry Spray*
- 3 *Yds. – 1 3/8" Cranberry Wired Ribbon*
- 1 – 1 1/2" *Lavender/ Celadon Sparrow*
- 1 *oz. – Spanish Moss*
- 5 *Pcs. – Floral Wire*
- *Glue (hot glue recommended)*

Instructions

1 Arrange three open roses and rosebuds along lower right side of wreath, as shown. Glue in place.

2 Glue a handful of moss near top left of wreath. Glue additional moss in and around roses at bottom of wreath.

3 Glue sparrow into moss at top left of wreath.

4 Cut rambling rose stems and berry sprays into smaller sections.

5 Glue three rose blooms and a few berry stems into moss near top of wreath. Glue remaining rambling rose and berry sections in and around large roses (*see drawing*).

6 Cut wired ribbon into seven 15" lengths. Form each length into 4" loops with a streamer (*see page 4*). Secure with wire. Glue two loops by bird. Fill in around flower arrangement with remaining loops. Glue to secure.

Sparrow

Rose blooms and berry sprays

Wired ribbon

Burgundy open roses and rosebuds

Wired ribbon

Rose stems and berry sprays

MAGNOLIA BASKET

Materials

- ❖ *1 – 13" Round Rattan Basket*
- ❖ *1 Stem – Pink Grand Magnolia*
- ❖ *1 Stem – 22" Pink Rambling Rose*
- ❖ *3 Stems – Plumb/Green Berry Spray*
- ❖ *Small Amount – Natural Raffia*
- ❖ *Small Amount – Spanish Moss*
- ❖ *3 oz. – Green Eucalyptus*
- ❖ *1 oz. – Natural Statice*
- ❖ *13 Pcs. – Mauve Curly Ting Ting*
- ❖ *7 – Mini Lotus Pods*
- ❖ *Glue (hot glue recommended)*

Instructions

1 Remove leaves from stem of magnolia. Cut stem about 1 1/2" from flower and glue, as shown, to left side of basket. Glue leaves to basket around flower.

2 Glue Spanish moss to base of handle on both sides of basket.

3 Wrap handle with raffia gluing at both ends. Make a single loop bow with raffia (*see page 5*), and glue to side of basket opposite flower.

4 Make four raffia loops. Glue one by raffia bow and the rest around magnolia, as shown.

5 Cut rambling rose, eucalyptus and berry spray into smaller sections. Arrange into moss on both sides of basket, referring to drawing.

6 Fill in arrangements with lotus pods, pieces of curly ting ting and statice. Glue in place.

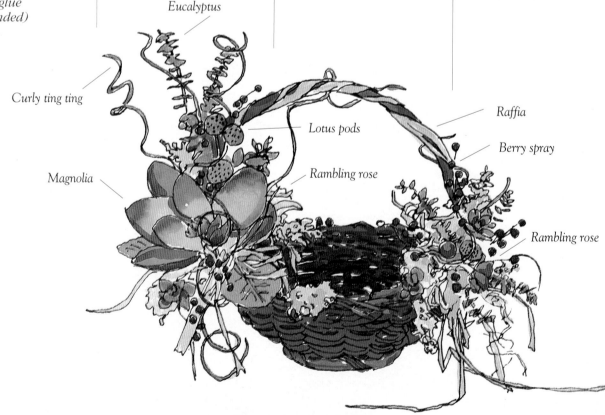

Eucalyptus

Curly ting ting

Lotus pods

Raffia

Berry spray

Magnolia

Rambling rose

Rambling rose

Rose Rattan Crown

Materials

- ❖ 1 – 32" Natural Flat Rattan Crown
- ❖ 3 Stems – Minuet Holland Rose
- ❖ 3 Stems – Minuet Rambling Roses
- ❖ 2 1/2 Yds. – 1 3/8" Pink/White, Wired Ribbon
- ❖ Glue (hot glue recommended)

Instructions

1 Arrange three large roses at bottom center of crown. Add smaller roses around large roses with some extending across lower edge of crown. Glue all roses in place.

2 Cut fourteen lengths of ribbon, varying lengths from 3" to 16".

3 Arrange ribbon lengths on rattan crown as shown in photograph. Weave ribbon throughout roses beginning at center. Cut ends at an angle.

Ribbon

Mauve Green Swag

Materials

- ❖ 1 – 29" Natural Grapevine Swag
- ❖ 2 – Grape Ivy Sprays
- ❖ 1 – Burgundy Peony Stem
- ❖ 2 – Burgundy Wild Rose Stems
- ❖ 2 1/2 Yds. – 1 3/8" Celadon Moire Ribbon
- ❖ 2 1/2 Yds. – 1 1/2" Mauve Moire Ribbon
- ❖ 5 Pcs. – Floral Wire
- ❖ Glue (hot glue recommended)

Instructions

1 Glue burgundy peony bloom to upper left of swag about 9" from end.

2 Arrange wild rose stems below peony, pointing in opposite directions (*See photo*). Glue in place.

3 Arrange one grape ivy spray at center of swag, under wild roses. Place second grape spray to left of peony pointing upward.

4 Placing 1/2 yard lengths of mauve and celadon ribbons together, make a double loop (with celadon on outside), securing ends with wire (*see page 4*).

5 Using 3/4 yard lengths of both colors ribbon make another double loop with 4" – 5" streamers. Repeat with one yard of both ribbons, making same size loops and long streamers.

6 Glue smallest ribbon loop at bottom of arrangement below peony. Glue loop with short streamers at top left of peony bloom.

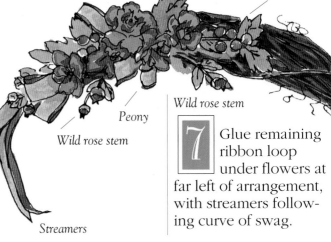

Grape ivy spray

Peony

Wild rose stem

Wild rose stem

Streamers

7 Glue remaining ribbon loop under flowers at far left of arrangement, with streamers following curve of swag.

ROSE TRIO BASKET

Materials

- 1– 14" Round Rattan Basket
- 3 – Minuet Holland Roses
- 1 Stem – 27 1/2" Grape Ivy Spray
- 1 Stem – 31 1/2" Grape Ivy
- Small Amount – Natural Statice
- Small Amount – Spanish Moss
- 2 Pcs. – Dried Mehogni Pods
- 3 Pcs. – Floral Wire
- Glue (hot glue recommended)

Instructions

1 Glue Spanish moss halfway around rim of basket and across top of handle as shown.

2 Twist grape ivy along handle of basket. Glue in place.

3 Cut grape ivy spray into pieces and secure along edge of basket as shown.

4 Glue mehogni pods to right side of basket on each side of handle.

5 Glue one rose to lower right side of handle and two more to rim of basket on right side. Use wire or glue to secure.

6 Fill in arrangement with statice and additional moss, as desired.

Grape ivy and Spanish moss

Mehogni pod

Starburst Rose Basket

Materials

- ❖ 1 – 10" Round Rattan Basket
- ❖ 6 – Minuet Holland Roses
- ❖ 1/3 Pkg. – Green Eucalyptus
- ❖ 1 – 18 1/2" Grape Ivy Spray
- ❖ 7 Pcs. – Mauve Curly Ting Ting
- ❖ 3 – Dried Mehogni Pods
- ❖ Small Amount – Spanish Moss
- ❖ 1 – Floral Foam Block
- ❖ Glue (hot glue recommended)

Instructions

1 Glue floral foam into bottom of basket, trimming to fit as needed. Cover with Spanish moss, gluing to secure.

2 Cut grape ivy spray in two sections

3 Arrange roses and grape ivy spray into foam and secure. *Refer to drawing.*

4 Add mehogni pods as shown. Fill in arrangement with eucalyptus and curly mauve ting ting. Glue in place.

Rose

Grape ivy

Eucalyptus

Mehogni pods are shown center front

Punch Bowl Wreath

Materials

- ❖ *1 – 18" Natural Hollow Wreath*
- ❖ *2 Stems – 27 1/2" Grape Ivy Spray*
- ❖ *2 Stems – 26" Burgundy Wild Roses*
- ❖ *2 oz. – Spanish Moss*
- ❖ *Glue (hot glue recommended)*

Instructions

1 Cut grape ivy sprays into sections.

2 Arrange spray sections around wreath, alternating with roses. Glue in place.

3 Fill in with Spanish moss.

Grape ivy spray

Burgundy wild rose

Note: Place flat on table to use as centerpiece or with punch bowl.